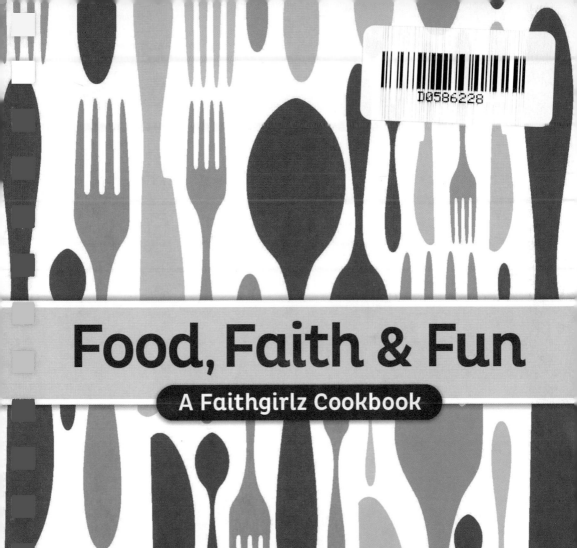

Food, Faith & Fun

A Faithgirlz Cookbook

The Faithgirlz Promise

I promise to always . . .

Focus on my inner beauty.

Remember that God loves me always.

Love myself the way God made me.

Look at others' gifts without jealousy.

Treat other people the way I want to be treated.

Love my neighbor.

Forgive others when they sin against me.

Love my enemies.

Seek God's will in all that I do.

Focus on the inner beauty of others.

So we fix our eyes not on
what is seen, but on what is
unseen, since what is seen
is temporary, but what is
unseen is eternal.

— 2 Corinthians 4:18

faiThGirLz!™
the beauty of believing

Food, Faith & Fun

A Faithgirlz Cookbook

ZONDERkidz

ZONDERVAN.com/
AUTHORTRACKER
follow your favorite authors

ZONDERKIDZ

Food, Faith, and Fun
Copyright © 2012 by Zonderkidz

Requests for information should be addressed to:

Zondervan, 5300 *Patterson Ave. S.E., Grand Rapids, Michigan 49530*

ISBN: 978–0–310–72–316–5

Library of Congress Cataloging-in-Publication Data
 Food, faith, and fun : a Faithgirlz! Cookbook.
          p.   cm.
      Includes index.
      ISBN 978-0-310-72316-5 (softcover)
      1. Cooking--Juvenile literature. 2. Food--Religious aspects--Christianity--
Juvenile literature. I. Title: Faithgirlz! Cookbook. II. Title: Food, faith, and fun.
TX652.5.F645 2012
641.5--dc23   2011053067

All Scripture quotations, unless otherwise indicated, are taken from the Holy Bible,
New International Version®, NIV®. Copyright © 1973, 1978, 1984, 2011 by Biblica, Inc.™
Used by permission. All rights reserved worldwide.

Any Internet addresses (websites, blogs, etc.) and telephone numbers in this book
are offered as a resource. They are not intended in any way to be or imply an
endorsement by Zondervan, nor does Zondervan vouch for the content of these
sites and numbers for the life of this book.

Some recipes originally appeared in *Focus on the Family Clubhouse* magazine.

Zonderkidz is a trademark of Zondervan.

Editor: Kim Childress
Design & art direction: Kris Nelson
Text composition: Matthew Van Zomeren
Recipe testing: Ron and Karen Nickel
Recipe photography: Ron Nickel Photography
Stock photography: Superstock, Corbis, Shutterstock, iStock

Printed in China

12 13 14 15 16 17 / LPC / 20 19 18 17 16 15 14 13 12 11 10 9 8 7 6 5 4 3 2 1

Table of Contents

About This Book

When you sit down at the dinner table with your family, you probably bow your head, close your eyes, and take a moment to say thank you to God for everything he has provided. Of all the blessings God provides — a home, a loving family, a warm bed — one of the most important blessings is food. Without all the nutrients you get from a crisp salad, a juicy burger, or a giant bowl of cereal, your body couldn't function.

The Bible says that your body is a temple of the Holy Spirit. You wouldn't go into a church and knock over the pulpit, get scuff marks all over the pews, and spill a drink on the carpet, right? God wants you to honor your body in the same way you honor his holy places, and that means getting up and moving instead of lying on the couch in front of the television . . . and filling your stomach with good food instead of junk.

When God created the world, he filled it with delicious foods to eat. Why eat the same old mac 'n' cheese from a box when there are so many delicious (and nutritious!) new tastes to explore? Good food will keep your body working and growing the way it should.

But food isn't just about putting fuel into your body. Food is also about the time it takes to prepare it and the experience of being in the kitchen with your friends and family. Food is about working to create the meal you will enjoy together. Food is about the memories you make with one another.

As you explore all the new foods and flavors in this book, don't think of the recipes as foods to make on the run. These are foods to enjoy making and eating with people you love. There are entrées and salads for family dinners, ice-cold smoothies for hot days sitting on the porch with your friends, and special desserts for the most important holidays. Grab a few of your Faithgirlz friends, throw on an apron, and start experimenting!

Cooking Tips and Instructions

Before you start cooking, be sure to ask a parent for permission — you don't want to use up all the flour if your mom was planning to make cookies later! Then wash your hands with soap and hot water, put on an apron to protect your clothes, and tie your hair back so it doesn't fall in the food.

When you're ready to begin, take a minute to read all the way through the recipe first, so you know what's coming. You don't want to get to step three of the instructions and discover that you're out of an important ingredient!

Next, gather all the equipment and ingredients you'll need. Wash, chop, and shred any fruits or vegetables you can before you get started. Grease any baking sheets you're going to need. When you're in the middle of cooking a complicated recipe, you'll be glad you don't have to worry about preparing the ingredients!

When you're cooking on the stove, make sure you turn the pan handles to the side. You wouldn't want to knock the pans over by mistake! If you're stirring a pan on the stove, keep a firm grip on the pan's handle. And always use oven mitts when you're taking hot dishes out of the oven.

Make sure you're always working on a clean surface. You don't want any germs from the kitchen counter spreading to your food! If you're working with raw meat, make sure to clean the cutting board, knife, your hands, and anything else the meat has touched before proceeding with the recipe. And once you're done cooking, it's important to clean up. Wash all the pans, bowls, spoons, and knives you've used in hot, soapy water, and put all the ingredients back in the cupboard or refrigerator.

If you're not confident chopping veggies with sharp knives or handling hot pans, ask your mom or dad to show you how to do this safely. After trying out a few recipes, you'll be a cooking pro!

Everything that lives and moves about will be food for you.
Just as i gave you the green plants, I now give you everything.
— **Genesis 9:3**

So whether you eat or drink or whatever you do, do it all for the glory of God.
— **1 Corinthians 10:31**

Do you not know that your bodies are temples of the Holy Spirit, who is in you,
whom you have received from God? You are not your own; you were bought at a price.
Therefore honor God with your bodies.
— **1 Corinthians 6:19 – 20**

He provides food for those who fear him; he remembers his covenant forever.
— **Psalm 111:5**

The Lord upholds all who fall and lifts up all who are bowed down.
The eyes of all look to you, and you give them their food at the proper time.
You open your hand and satisfy the desires of every living thing.
— **Psalm 145:14 – 16**

munchies

So whether
you eat or drink
or whatever you do,
do it all for the
glory of God.

—1 Corinthians 10:31

Peanutty-Chocolate Pretzels

You'll Need

- 1 cup creamy peanut butter
- 2 teaspoons butter, room temperature
- ⅔ cup powdered sugar
- ¾ cup light brown sugar
- ½ teaspoon vanilla extract
- 2 cups pretzels, lightly crushed
- 2 cups chocolate chips

Directions

1. Beat peanut butter and butter together until smooth and creamy.

2. Beat in powdered sugar, light brown sugar, and vanilla extract until well mixed. Add more powdered sugar until filling can hold its shape.

3. Fold in broken pretzel pieces. Pieces must be very small so balls can be shaped easily.

4. Form peanut butter-pretzel mixture into balls.

5. Place balls on sheet pan covered in wax paper and refrigerate until ready to dip in chocolate.

6. Melt chocolate chips in microwave for 30 seconds, stir, and melt an additional 30 seconds if needed. It may be necessary to reheat if the chocolate gets hard.

7. Using a fork, dip each ball in chocolate.

8. Return dipped peanut butter balls to sheet pan and refrigerate until chocolate sets.

Carrot Cake Cookies

You'll Need

- 1 cup all-purpose whole-wheat flour
- ½ cup old-fashioned oats
- ½ cup pure maple syrup
- ¼ cup butter, melted
- ½ teaspoon vanilla extract
- 1 teaspoon baking powder
- ½ teaspoon baking soda
- ½ teaspoon ground ginger
- 1 teaspoon ground cinnamon
- ½ teaspoon ground nutmeg
- ½ cup grated carrots
- ½ cup raisins
- ½ cup flaked coconut
- ½ cup chopped walnuts

Directions

1 Preheat oven to 325° Fahrenheit.

2 Combine all ingredients in a large bowl. Mix well until batter is blended evenly.

3 Use a tablespoon to portion cookies on greased baking sheet, approximately 1 – 2 inches apart.

4 Bake cookies for 18 minutes or until cooked through.

5 Remove cookies from baking sheet and allow to cool on a wire rack.

From: Tonya

Granola and Yogurt Parfait

You'll Need

3   cups old-fashioned oats
1   cup dried fruit (cranberries, apples, and/or apricots)
1   cup nuts, chopped (pecan, almonds, or walnuts)
3   tablespoons brown sugar
¾   teaspoon ground cinnamon
½   teaspoon ground ginger
¼   teaspoon salt
⅓   cup honey
2   tablespoons vegetable oil
3   cups vanilla yogurt
1   cup strawberries
1   cup blueberries or raspberries

Directions

1 Preheat oven to 300° Fahrenheit.

2 Combine oats, dried fruit, nuts, brown sugar, cinnamon, ginger, and salt in large bowl.

3 Stir honey and oil together in saucepan over medium heat until blended well.

4 Pour honey mixture over oat mixture. Mix well.

5 Spread mixture onto greased baking sheet.

6 Bake for 10 minutes. Take out and stir.

7 Repeat baking and stirring 3 more times.

8 Let granola cool.

9 Place a scoop of yogurt in bottom of 4 large, clear glasses. Add a scoop of granola to each glass, and then a layer of fresh fruit. Repeat layering until each glass is full.

Fruit Flower

You'll Need

Small plate

Peanut butter

1 apple with peel, cored and sliced

1 strawberry, stem removed

Directions

1 Spread peanut butter directly onto plate.

2 Wash strawberry and place in center of peanut butter.

3 Arrange apple slices around strawberry in a flower-petal pattern.

From: Abigail

Cinnamon and Spice Fruit Dip

You'll Need

- 1 cup heavy whipping cream
- 1 teaspoon vanilla extract
- 1 teaspoon white granulated sugar
- ¼ cup brown sugar
- ¼ teaspoon ground cinnamon
- Dash of nutmeg

Directions

1 Pour cold whipping cream into cold mixing bowl. Add vanilla and sugar. Beat with electric mixer on high until soft peaks form.

2 Sprinkle brown sugar, cinnamon, and nutmeg onto whipped cream and mix in slowly.

3 Serve as dip for strawberries, raspberries, and blueberries, as well as pear, apple, and banana slices.

Veggie Dip

You'll Need

⅔ cup sour cream

⅔ cup mayonnaise

1 tablespoon seasoned salt

1 tablespoon dried dill weed

1 tablespoon dried onion flakes

1 tablespoon dried parsley flakes

Directions

1 Mix ingredients in medium-sized bowl.

2 Serve with fresh-cut vegetables like carrots, broccoli, cauliflower, radishes, and bell peppers.

Celery Stick Butterfly

You'll Need

Stalk of celery
Peanut butter
Pretzels

Directions

1 Wash one stalk of celery and spread with peanut butter.

2 Stick two regular pretzels into peanut butter for wings.

3 Place two small pretzel pieces at one end of celery for antennae.

From: Abby

Cheese Ball

You'll Need

2   ounces cream cheese
2   cups shredded cheddar cheese
1   teaspoon red bell pepper, finely chopped
1   tablespoon green bell pepper, finely chopped
1   tablespoon pimiento, finely chopped
1   tablespoon onion, finely chopped
2   tablespoons Worcestershire sauce
1   teaspoon lemon juice
    Dash of salt
    Dash of cayenne pepper
½   cup walnuts, chopped

Directions

1   Thoroughly mix all ingredients, except walnuts, in medium-sized bowl.

2   Shape cheese mixture into large ball and roll in chopped walnuts until evenly covered. Serve with crackers, pretzels, and carrot sticks.

Fried Dill Pickles

You'll need

1 egg, beaten

1 cup milk

1 tablespoon all-purpose flour

1 tablespoon Worcestershire sauce

3½ cups all-purpose flour

¾ teaspoon salt

¾ teaspoon ground black pepper

1 32-ounce jar sliced dill pickles, drained

1 quart vegetable oil for deep frying

Directions

1 In small bowl, mix egg, milk, 1 tablespoon flour, and Worcestershire sauce.

2 In a separate bowl, stir together 3½ cups flour, salt, and pepper.

3 Heat oil to 350° Fahrenheit in deep fryer or heavy, deep skillet. Dip pickle slices into milk mixture, and then into flour mixture.

4 Carefully place pickles into hot oil. Fry in several batches to avoid overcrowding. When done, pickles will float to surface and turn golden brown.

5 Remove with slotted spoon and drain on paper towels. These are delicious dipped in ranch or blue-cheese dressing!

From: Kathleen

Spinach Balls

You'll Need

- 1¾ cup bread crumbs, recipe below
- 1 pound frozen, chopped spinach, thawed
- 5 eggs
- 1 large onion
- ½ cup butter, melted
- ¾ cup parmesan cheese
- 2 cloves garlic, minced
- ½ teaspoon dried thyme
- ½ teaspoon cayenne pepper

Directions

1 Preheat oven to 350° Fahrenheit.

2 Press fully thawed spinach into colander to remove excess water.

3 Mix with remaining ingredients by hand in large bowl.

4 Form mixture into 1-inch balls and place on baking sheet.

5 Bake 20 to 25 minutes, or until firm. Remove from oven and arrange on tray before serving.

Bread Crumbs
You'll Need

Bread slices, any variety

Directions

1 If only fresh bread is available, place in 300° Fahrenheit oven for 10 to 15 minutes until dry, turning every 5 minutes for even baking.

2 Place dry bread into food processor and pulse until only crumbs are left.

Hummus

You'll Need

1 15-ounce can chickpeas (garbanzo beans)
½ teaspoon ground cumin
3 tablespoons tahini
2 cloves garlic, minced
¼ cup olive oil
¼ cup fresh lemon juice
½ teaspoon paprika
¼ teaspoon cayenne pepper
   Salt to taste

Directions

1 Drain chickpeas, but reserve some of the liquid.

2 Place ingredients in blender or food processor.

3 Add some of the reserved liquid from chickpeas and blend until paste forms.

4 Chill and serve with flatbread or crackers.

Homemade Hot Pretzels

You'll Need

1 tablespoon active, dry yeast
1½ cups warm water
1 teaspoon salt
1 tablespoon white granulated sugar
4 cups all-purpose flour
½ cup butter, melted
¼ teaspoon kosher salt

Directions

1 Preheat oven to 425° Fahrenheit and lightly spray 2 cookie sheets with cooking spray.

2 Dissolve yeast in warm water. Pour into large bowl and add salt and sugar, stirring until thoroughly mixed.

3 Add flour to bowl, 1 cup at a time. Mix until blended.

4 Ask a parent to help you knead the dough for 5 minutes.

5 On floured surface, roll out dough into ½-inch thick rectangle.

6 Cut into 15 1-inch-wide strips. Arrange strips into pretzel shape.

7 Place pretzel-shaped dough on greased cookie sheets. Brush with melted butter and sprinkle with kosher salt. Bake for 10 to 15 minutes, or until pretzels are golden brown.

From: Sharon

Honey-Coated Almonds

You'll Need

¼ cup honey
1 tablespoon flaxseed meal
1 tsp cinnamon
1 cup almonds
Cooking spray

Directions

1 Mix honey, flaxseed, and cinnamon in medium-sized bowl.

2 Add almonds and coat thoroughly with mixture.

3 Lightly coat baking pan with cooking spray.

4 Spread almonds on pan and place in freezer.

5 Before serving, thaw for a few minutes.

From: Isabella

Krazy Krunch

You'll Need

2   cups applesauce
½   cup crispy rice cereal
1   banana
½   cup small oat-ring cereal
    Dash of cinnamon
    Nuts (optional)

Directions

1   In small bowl, stir crispy rice cereal into applesauce.

2   Cut banana into small, bite-size pieces and add to mixture.

3   Divide mixture evenly between 4 cereal bowls.

4   Sprinkle with oat-ring cereal, cinnamon, and nuts.

5   Add more cereal for a "krazy krunch!"

From: Karah

Peanut-Butter Bumbles

You'll Need

¼   cup creamy peanut butter
½   cup powdered sugar
1   tablespoon butter, softened
½   cup graham cracker crumbs
¼   cup chocolate chips
½   cup sliced almonds
      Extra chocolate chips
      Plastic ziplock bag

Directions

1 Mix together peanut butter, powdered sugar, butter, and graham cracker crumbs.

2 Shape peanut butter into ovals to serve as the bumblebees' bodies and place them onto greased cookie sheet.

3 Melt chocolate chips in small saucepan over low heat; then pour melted chocolate into plastic ziplock bag.

4 With scissors, snip off tiny corner of bag; then squeeze bag to drizzle chocolate stripes onto bee bodies.

5 Create wings with sliced almonds. Make eyes with extra chocolate chips.

6 Allow chocolate to dry; then taste and "bee stung" with flavor!

From: Katie

Peanut Clusters

You'll Need

Wax paper
1 pound white chocolate chips
½ cup peanut butter
1 cup dry-roasted peanuts
1 cup small marshmallows
1½ cups crispy rice cereal

Directions

1 Place large sheets of wax paper on counter or cookie sheet.

2 Melt white chocolate chips in medium-sized saucepan over low heat. Once melted, stir in peanut butter.

3 Turn off heat; then add remaining ingredients. Stir until combined.

4 Drop large spoonfuls of mixture onto wax paper and let sit for 1 hour to harden.

From: Sharon

Toffee Tarts

You'll Need

⅓ cup brown sugar

3 tablespoons cornstarch

½ cup heavy cream

2 egg yolks

1½ cups milk

¼ cup toffee bits

1 banana

6 4-ounce graham cracker pie crusts

2 tablespoons toffee bits (for topping)

Directions

1 Mix brown sugar and cornstarch in large bowl.

2 Blend in cream and egg yolks. Add milk; then pour mixture into saucepan.

3 Over medium heat, stir constantly 5 to 10 minutes until mixture thickens.

4 Pour pudding into bowl. (If pudding is lumpy, pour it through a strainer.)

5 Stir in ¼ cup toffee bits.

6 Cover bowl with plastic wrap and refrigerate until cool.

7 Slice banana into ½-inch rounds and place three slices in bottom of each piecrust.

8 Fill pie crusts with pudding and top with 2 tablespoons toffee bits.

9 Refrigerate for one hour and slice to serve.

Caramel Popcorn

You'll Need

- 1 cup brown sugar
- ½ cup (1 stick) butter
- ¼ cup light corn syrup
- 1 teaspoon vanilla extract
- 1 teaspoon baking soda
- 10 cups popped, unbuttered popcorn

Directions

1 Preheat oven to 250° Fahrenheit and line two cookie sheets with parchment paper.

2 Melt brown sugar, butter, corn syrup, and vanilla in saucepan; then boil over medium heat for three minutes.

3 Remove from heat and stir in 1 teaspoon baking soda.

4 Pour syrup over popped popcorn. Mix well. Spread coated popcorn onto prepared cookie sheets. Bake for 1 hour, stirring every 15 minutes.

5 Remove popcorn from oven and pour into large bowl.

Lazy Lions

You'll Need

- Cream cheese
- 1 bagel, sliced
- Stick pretzels
- 2 small, round butter-flavored crackers
- Diced celery
- 2 small round pretzels

Directions

1 Spread cream cheese on bagel halves.

2 Press stick pretzels into cheese around outside edges of each bagel to make lion's mane. Place a cracker in center of bagel as a nose.

3 Make eyes out of celery pieces; then place round pretzel under nose as a mouth. Enjoy!

From: Nicole

Volcano Cookies

You'll Need

- 3 tablespoons cocoa
- 3 tablespoons butter
- 1 cup white granulated sugar
- 2 eggs
- 1½ cups all-purpose flour
- 1 teaspoon vanilla extract
- 1½ teaspoons baking powder
- ¼ teaspoon salt
  Powdered sugar

Directions

1 Mix ingredients, except powdered sugar, in large bowl and chill dough for 1 hour.

2 Preheat oven to 350° Fahrenheit.

3 Roll dough into balls.

4 Pour liberal amount of powdered sugar into a medium-sized bowl and toss cookie-dough balls in sugar until evenly covered.

5 Place balls on greased cookie sheet and bake for 10 minutes, or until firm.

6 Remove cookies from oven and cool on baking sheet for 5 minutes before moving cookies to wire rack to cool fully.

From: Savannah

drinks

"Everyone who drinks this water
will be thirsty again, but
whoever drinks the water
I give them will never thirst.
Indeed, the water I give them
will become in them a spring of
water welling up to eternal life."

— John 4:13–14

Berry-licious Smoothie

You'll Need

½ cup blueberries
⅓ cup milk
3 or 4 ice cubes
1 tablespoon honey
¾ cup of vanilla yogurt

Directions

1 Place ingredients in blender and mix well.

2 Pour into tall glasses and serve with straws. Enjoy!

From: Paige

Orange Cream Dream

You'll Need

½ cup vanilla yogurt
1 cup orange juice, chilled
1 tablespoon honey

Directions

1 Add ingredients to blender and mix thoroughly, until honey dissolves.

2 Pour into a glass and enjoy your creamy drink!

From: Shawna

Homemade Lemonade

You'll Need

6   lemons
2   cups white granulated sugar
1   gallon water
2   lemon rinds

Directions

1   Squeeze lemons in a citrus juicer, setting aside 2 rinds. Pour juice into a large pitcher.

2   Add sugar to pitcher and stir well. Add water to pitcher and stir well.

3   Add lemon rinds to pitcher. Cover and refrigerate for 24 hours before serving.

Sour Power Punch

You'll Need

1	teaspoon lemon juice
1	teaspoon lime juice
1	cup raspberries
1	cup ice cubes
1	cup orange juice
4	teaspoons white granulated sugar

Directions

1 Add ingredients to blender and mix well.

2 Serve in a tall glass with a straw.

From: Emily

Green Smoothie

You'll Need

1   apple, cut, cored, and peeled
1   cup fresh spinach
½   banana
¼   cup water
3   strawberries, without stems
3   peach slices
3   ice cubes
1   tablespoon honey
    Blueberries, for topping

Directions

1 Thoroughly wash all fruits and veggies.

2 In blender, combine apple, spinach, banana, and water. Blend until smooth.

3 Add strawberries and peaches. Blend well.

4 Add ice cubes and honey. Blend until ice is crushed and honey is mixed in.

5 Pour into glasses and top with blueberries. Enjoy!

From: Stephanie

Comfy Cozy Chai

You'll Need

2   cups water
¼   cup honey
4   black tea bags
½   teaspoon vanilla extract
1   cinnamon stick
1   teaspoon ground cloves
¼   teaspoon ground ginger
¼   teaspoon ground cardamom
⅛   teaspoon ground nutmeg
2   cups milk

Directions

1 In saucepan, bring water to a boil.

2 Add honey, tea bags, vanilla, and spices.

3 Reduce heat and simmer for 5 minutes.

4 Add milk and heat to a near boil.

5 Remove from heat and serve in your favorite mug.

Oreo Milkshake

You'll Need

1   cup milk
2   scoops vanilla ice cream
     Oreo cookies

Directions

1   Combine ingredients in blender and mix until smooth.

2   Pour into a glass and enjoy!

From: Sydnie

Peanut Butter Fudge Shake

Directions

1 Combine ingredients in blender and mix until smooth.

2 Serve in a tall glass with a straw and a spoon.

From: Katie

You'll Need

3 scoops vanilla ice cream

⅓ cup peanut butter

¼ cup fudge sauce

½ cup milk

Mulled Cider

You'll Need

2   quarts apple cider
¼   cup brown sugar
2   cinnamon sticks
1   teaspoon whole cloves
⅛   teaspoon ground ginger
1   orange slice

Directions

1 Place ingredients in slow cooker or large pot.

2 Heat until warm.

3 Reduce heat and simmer.

4 Serve warm in a mug and savor!

From: Taylor

Snowman Hot Tub

You'll Need

3   scoops vanilla ice cream
1   package hot chocolate mix
2   pretzel sticks
6   mini hard-covered chocolate candies

Directions

1   Prepare hot chocolate according to package directions.

2   Place three scoops of ice cream in mug, one scoop on top of the next to form snowman's body.

3   Insert pretzels into middle scoop of ice cream, one on each side, to make arms.

4   Add hard-covered chocolate candies to top ice cream scoop to give your snowman a face.

5   Slowly pour hot chocolate into mug, and watch your snowman melt away!

From: Sarah

salads

Then God said, "Let the land produce vegetation: seed-bearing plants and trees on the land that bear fruit with seed in it, according to their various kinds." And it was so.

— Genesis 1:11

Mandarin Orange Salad

You'll Need

- ½ cup sliced almonds
- 1¾ tablespoon white granulated sugar
- 1 head iceberg lettuce
- ½ bunch romaine lettuce
- 2 medium stalks celery, chopped
- 3 green onions, thinly sliced
- 1 11-ounce can mandarin oranges

Directions

1 Combine almonds and sugar in saucepan. Dissolve sugar over medium heat stirring almonds constantly until they're glazed with sugar.

2 Toss iceberg and romaine lettuce in large bowl. Add celery, green onions, oranges, and glazed almonds.

3 Refrigerate before serving.

Dressing

You'll Need

- ¼ cup olive oil
  Dash hot-pepper sauce
- 4 tablespoons sugar
- 4 tablespoons distilled vinegar
- 2 tablespoons parsley, chopped
- ½ teaspoon salt
  Dash ground black pepper

Directions

1 Mix ingredients in small bowl.

2 Toss dressing with salad greens prior to serving.

Perfect Potato Salad

You'll Need

2½ pounds small red-skinned
   potatoes
3   eggs, hard-boiled
1   cup mayonnaise
½   medium onion, diced
1   green onion, thinly sliced
2   stalks celery, chopped
1   teaspoon salt
½   teaspoon ground black pepper

Directions

1 Fill large pot with water and add potatoes.
  Bring to boil over high heat.

2 Boil for 15 to 20 minutes, until potatoes
  are tender but not falling apart. Ask an
  adult to help you drain water.

3 When potatoes are cool, cut into cubes.

4 Place eggs in small saucepan and cover
  with cold water. Bring water to boil; then
  remove pan from stovetop.

5 Let eggs stand in hot water for 15 minutes.
  Then remove from water, peel off shells,
  and chop up eggs.

6 Combine eggs and potatoes in large bowl,
  mixing gently with a rubber spatula. (Be
  careful — you don't want mashed-potato
  salad!)

7 Mix remaining ingredients in a small bowl;
  then fold mixture into potatoes and eggs.
  Cover bowl and refrigerate at least 3 hours
  before serving.

Tuna Salad

You'll Need

2   5-ounce cans tuna, drained

1   tablespoon sweet relish

2   tablespoons mayonnaise

1   teaspoon honey mustard

⅛   teaspoon curry powder (optional)

Directions

1   Mix tuna with relish, mayonnaise, mustard, and curry powder in medium-sized bowl.

2   Enjoy as a stand-alone treat, served over lettuce, or on a sandwich with your favorite bread.

Lemony Salad Dressing

Directions

1 Cut lemons in half and remove seeds. Squeeze juice from lemons and combine with oil in large bowl.

2 Add vinegar, salt, and pepper. Use wire whisk to mix ingredients.

3 Add whole, crushed clove of garlic to oil mixture for added flavor.

4 Toss lemon dressing with torn lettuce and serve.

5 Store leftover dressing in a jar in refrigerator.

You'll Need

1 cup olive oil

2 lemons

¼ cup distilled vinegar

½ teaspoon salt

¼ teaspoon ground black pepper

1 clove garlic, crushed

Greek Pasta Salad

Dressing
You'll Need

⅔ cup olive oil

3 tablespoons red-wine vinegar

1 teaspoon dried basil

1 green onion, chopped

¼ teaspoon dried oregano

2 tablespoons parmesan cheese

1 teaspoon white granulated sugar

½ teaspoon salt

¼ teaspoon ground black pepper

Salad
You'll Need

1 pound penne pasta

1 cup black olives, sliced

1 cup feta cheese, crumbled

Directions

1 Cook pasta according to package directions, until al dente. Ask an adult to help you drain pasta; then pour it into a large bowl.

2 While pasta cools, mix ingredients for dressing in a small bowl.

3 Mix olives and feta cheese into cooled pasta. Pour dressing over pasta and chill at least 1 hour before serving.

Sparkling Fruit Compote

You'll Need

1 large orange
2 kiwifruit
1 15-ounce can sliced pears, drained
1 large bottle sparkling apple cider
  Sherbet or frozen yogurt (any flavor)
  Clear juice glasses

Directions

1 Peel orange. Slice horizontally to make circles and remove seeds; then cut circles in halves or quarters to fit glass.

2 Peel kiwifruit; slice horizontally in circles.

3 Layer slices of orange, kiwifruit, and pears in clear glasses and chill in refrigerator.

4 Before serving, pour chilled sparkling cider over fruit.

5 Top with a spoonful of sherbet or frozen yogurt to delight the senses!

Strawberry Spinach Salad

Strawberry Spinach Salad

You'll Need

4   cups spinach, rinsed and torn into pieces
2   cups strawberries, sliced

Directions

1   In a large bowl, toss together the spinach and strawberries.

Poppy Seed Vinaigrette

You'll Need

2   tablespoons olive oil
2   tablespoons apple cider vinegar
1   tablespoon lemon juice
1½   teaspoons white granulated sugar
½   tablespoon poppy seeds

Directions

1   In medium bowl, whisk all ingredients together until blended.

2   Pour over salad.

3   Toss until salad is thoroughly coated.

Waterloo Salad

You'll Need

1   20-ounce can pineapple chunks, drained
1   11-ounce can mandarin orange pieces, drained
1   cup shredded coconut
1   cup sour cream
1   cup mini marshmallows

Directions

1   Mix ingredients in a large bowl.
2   Cover bowl and chill in refrigerator until ready to serve.

main courses

You prepare
a table before me ...

— Psalm 23:5

Pig in a Hole

You'll Need

Round cookie cutter
2 eggs
1 sausage patty
1 slice of whole-grain bread
Butter
Salt and pepper
1 slice cheddar cheese

Directions

1 Use cookie cutter to shape sausage patty.

2 Scramble eggs and cook till firm and fluffy.

3 Fry sausage in skillet, turning for even browning.

4 Toast slice of bread until evenly browned. Butter toast.

5 After washing and drying cookie cutter from step 1, use it to cut a hole in toast.

6 Fit fully cooked sausage patty into hole of toast.

7 Spoon scrambled eggs on top of sausage patty and toast. Add salt and pepper to taste.

8 Place cheddar cheese on top of eggs and top with buttered hole that was cut from toast.

9 Allow cheese to melt slightly and eat!

Zucchini Frittata

You'll Need

1 tablespoon olive oil
1 Zucchini, cut into thin
   slices
   Salt and pepper to taste
   Pinch of garlic powder
4 eggs, beaten
   Parmesan cheese, for
   topping

Directions

1 In a medium-sized frying pan,
   cook zucchini slices in olive oil
   over medium heat with a dash of
   salt, pepper, and garlic powder.

2 Flip slices with tongs and cook
   until zucchini looks clear.

4 Whisk eggs in separate bowl;
   then pour over zucchini. Cook on
   medium heat 5-7 minuites until
   frittata is set around the edge.

4 Cover, reduce heat to medium-
   low, and cook additional 5
   minutes, or until eggs are firm.

5 Remove pan from heat, keep
   covered, and let stand 5 more
   minutes.

6 Remove frittata with a spatula and
   serve with parmesan cheese.

From: Sarah

White Chicken Chili

You'll Need

6   boneless, skinless chicken breasts
1   large onion, finely chopped
3   tablespoons olive oil
1   4-ounce can chopped green chilies
1   4-ounce can of chopped jalapeños
1   tablespoon cumin
1   tablespoon oregano
1   tablespoon chili powder
1   tablespoon chopped garlic
4   15-ounce cans navy beans, drained
1   15-ounce can chili beans
4   cups of chicken broth
2½ cups shredded Monterey Jack cheese

Directions

1 Lightly season chicken breasts with salt and pepper.

2 Roast in 350° Fahrenheit oven for 35 minutes.

3 Let cool and chop into bite-size pieces. Set aside.

4 In a heavy pan, sauté onion in oil until transparent. Add chilies, jalapeños, and all spices and continue cooking for 5 minutes.

5 Add chicken and beans and stir well.

6 Slowly add broth.

7 After bringing mixture to boil, simmer for 1 hour.

8 Take off heat and stir in cheese until melted.

9 Serve with tortilla chips.

From: Mary

Bacon Wraps

You'll Need

Cream cheese
2 flour tortillas
Crumbled cooked bacon
Shredded cheese (any variety)
1 carrot, shredded

Directions

1 Spread a thin layer of cream cheese on tortillas.

2 Sprinkle on crumbled bacon, cheese, and carrots.

3 Roll up tortillas.

4 Cut into 1-inch pieces. Serve and enjoy.

From: Danielle

Guacamole Wraps

You'll Need

Guacamole

1 avocado
2 tablespoons salsa
2 tablespoons sour cream
⅛ teaspoon salt

Wraps

4 flour tortillas
1 cup lettuce, shredded
1 cup cooked chicken, chopped
Fresh guacamole
½ cup salsa
1 cup cheddar cheese, shredded
Tortilla chips

Directions

Guacamole

1 With an adult's help, cut avocado in half lengthwise. Remove pit with a spoon and scoop avocado flesh into medium-sized bowl. Discard skin.

2 Add salsa and mash avocado with a fork.

3 Stir in sour cream and salt.

Wraps

1 Sprinkle lettuce and chicken on a tortilla and top with guacamole, salsa, and cheese.

2 Fold up bottom of tortilla to cover part of filling. Then roll in from side, leaving top open. Repeat with remaining tortillas.

3 Serve with chips and salsa.

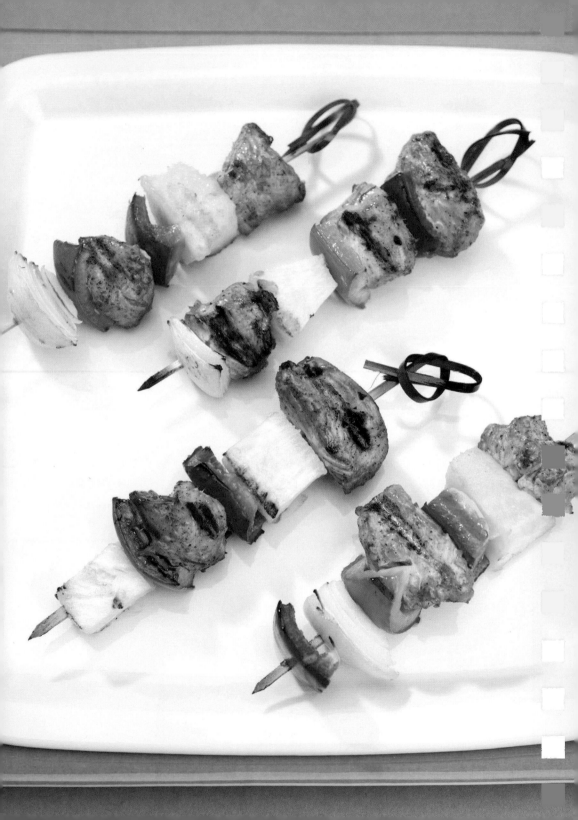

Turkey Kebab

You'll Need

Marinade

⅛ teaspoon ground black pepper
½ teaspoon kosher or sea salt
⅛ teaspoon ground allspice
⅛ teaspoon ground cinnamon
⅛ teaspoon ground cumin
½ tablespoon soy sauce
1 tablespoon lime juice
½ cup onion, minced
1 teaspoon grated lime peel (zest)

Kebabs

1 pound lean turkey-breast meat
1 onion
1 green pepper
1 red Pepper
1 20-ounce can pineapple chunks
   Kebab skewers

Directions

1 Mix ingredients for marinade in a large bowl. Cut kebab ingredients into 1-inch chunks.

2 Place turkey in marinade and refrigerate for 1 hour.

3 While turkey is marinating, soak bamboo skewers in water.

4 Thread marinated turkey and vegetable chunks onto soaked skewers.

5 Grill kebabs until turkey is cooked thoroughly.

Mango Chicken Quesadilla

You'll Need

2   flour tortillas
1   mango, peeled and thinly sliced
½   cup of grilled chicken, shredded
½   cup of Mexican cheese blend, shredded
1   tablespoon olive oil
    Salsa (optional)

Directions

1 Heat oil in nonstick skillet over medium heat.

2 Set one tortilla in skillet and top with shredded chicken, cheese, and mango slices. Top with second tortilla.

3 When cheese begins to melt, flip quesadilla and heat until second side begins to brown. Serve with salsa.

From: Rebecca

Enchiladas

You'll Need

1 pound lean ground turkey
1 packet taco seasoning
½ cup sour cream
1 10-ounce can nacho-cheese soup
  (or cheddar cheese soup)
½ cup milk
6 burrito-sized flour tortillas
1 16-ounce can refried beans
1 cup cooked rice
3 cups shredded cheddar cheese

Directions

1 Preheat oven to 350° Fahrenheit.

2 Brown ground turkey in skillet over medium heat, adding taco seasoning as directed on packet.

3 Combine sour cream, cheese soup, and milk in saucepan and heat, stirring until mixed well.

4 On tortillas, evenly layer refried beans, browned and seasoned ground turkey, half of the soup mixture, rice, and 1 cup of shredded cheese.

5 Roll tortillas tightly and place side by side in a 9" x 13" pan. Pour remaining soup mixture over enchiladas and sprinkle remaining cheddar cheese on top.

6 Bake enchiladas for 30 minutes, or until cheese is melted and golden brown.

Sweet and Sour Meatballs

Meatballs
You'll Need

    Cooking spray
1   pound lean ground beef
1¼ cups dried bread crumbs
4   large eggs
4   ounces milk
1⅓ cups grated parmesan cheese
½   medium onion, finely chopped
4   cloves fresh garlic, minced
2   tablespoons fresh parsley, finely chopped
¼   cup fresh basil, finely chopped

Sweet and Sour Sauce
You'll Need

1   16-ounce can jellied cranberry sauce
12 ounces chili sauce
2   tablespoons brown sugar
1   tablespoon lemon juice

Directions

1 Mix ingredients in a saucepan and simmer on low heat.

2 To serve, pour over baked meatballs.

Directions

1 Preheat oven to 350° Fahrenheit and spray a baking sheet with cooking spray.

2 Mix ingredients in a large bowl.

3 Hand-roll meatballs loosely into 1-inch balls and place on baking sheet. Bake for approximately 15 to 18 minutes, or until thoroughly cooked.

4 Remove from oven and place in covered bowl. Serve with Sweet and Sour Sauce.

Blackened Chicken

You'll Need

1   teaspoon paprika
4   teaspoons white granulated sugar, divided
1½ teaspoon salt, divided
1   teaspoon garlic powder
1   teaspoon dried thyme
1   teaspoon lemon pepper
1   teaspoon cayenne pepper
1   teaspoon ground black pepper, divided
4   boneless, skinless chicken breast halves
1⅓ cups mayonnaise
1   teaspoon water
2   teaspoons apple-cider vinegar

Directions

1 In a small bowl, combine paprika, 1 teaspoon sugar, 1 teaspoon salt, garlic powder, thyme, lemon pepper, cayenne pepper, and ¾ teaspoon black pepper.

2 Sprinkle mixed seasonings over both sides of chicken and set aside.

3 In another bowl, combine mayonnaise, water, vinegar, and remaining sugar, salt, and black pepper. Cover and chill 1 cup of mixture for serving. Save remaining sauce for basting.

4 With an adult's help, grill chicken, covered, over indirect heat for 4 to 6 minutes on each side, or until juices run clear, basting frequently with sauce.

5 Serve with chilled sauce for a zesty flavor!

From: Erika

Open-Faced Buns

You'll Need

8   hamburger buns
½   pound lean ground beef
2   tablespoons ketchup
4   tablespoons mayonnaise
1   tablespoon onion, minced
½   teaspoon mustard
⅛   teaspoon salt
⅛   teaspoon ground black pepper
4   tablespoons shredded cheddar cheese

Directions

1 Separate hamburger buns into halves (16 pieces).

2 Mix other ingredients in a large bowl.

3 Spread meat mixture evenly on each of the 16 hamburger bun halves.

4 Place buns, open-faced, on a baking sheet and broil in oven until meat is browned and thoroughly cooked.

5 Remove from oven and serve.

Red Beans, Sausage and Rice

You'll Need

½ tablespoon canola oil
1 small onion, diced
2 celery sticks, sliced
⅓ cup green bell pepper, diced
2 garlic cloves, minced
1 tablespoon Creole seasoning
12 ounces andouille (hot and spicy) sausage
1 tablespoon tomato paste
2 tablespoons fresh parsley, chopped
1 cup uncooked rice
2 cups chicken broth
2 bay leaves
1 15-ounce can kidney beans, drained and rinsed

Directions

1 Heat oil in a large skillet that has a lid. Sauté onion, celery, bell pepper, garlic, and ½ tablespoon of Creole seasoning over medium-high heat until tender.

2 Add sausage and cook until brown. Stir in tomato paste, parsley, and rice; cook 1 minute.

3 Add chicken broth, bay leaves, remaining Creole seasoning, and kidney beans. Mix well and bring to a boil over high heat.

4 Cover skillet, reduce heat to low, and cook until rice is done (about 20 minutes).

5 Remove from heat and let sit for a few minutes before serving.

Scotch Eggs

You'll Need

5   eggs
1   pound ground breakfast sausage
½   cup all-purpose flour
2   cups dried bread crumbs

Directions

1 Place five eggs in a single layer in a saucepan.

2 Cover eggs with cold water so that water is an inch or two above eggs.

3 Put saucepan on stove on high heat, and bring water to boil.

4 As soon as water begins to boil, reduce heat to low.

5 Let simmer for one minute, then remove pan from heat.

6 Cover saucepan and let sit for 12 minutes.

7 Remove eggs from water and let cool.

8 When eggs are cool, remove shells.

9 Evenly divide breakfast sausage into 5 portions.

10 Roll an egg in flour.

11 Evenly wrap one portion of sausage around floured egg, ensuring that egg is covered completely.

12 Roll egg/sausage ball in bread crumbs.

13 Repeat for remaining eggs and sausage.

14 Bake in a 375° Fahrenheit oven for 30 minutes or until bread crumbs are golden-brown.

Mashed Potatoes Pizzazz

You'll Need

8-10 medium potatoes, peeled

8   ounces cream cheese

8   ounces sour cream

1   teaspoon salt

1   teaspoon onion salt

4   tablespoons butter, cut into ½-tablespoon chunks

    Paprika

Directions

1 Peel potatoes and cut into ½-inch cubes. Place in saucepan and cover with water.

2 Bring water to boil and cook potatoes until very soft and easily pierced with a fork.

3 Preheat oven to 350˚ Fahrenheit.

4 Whip potatoes, cream cheese, and sour cream with an electric mixer until smooth (or mash with a potato masher). Stir in salt and onion salt.

5 Spoon potatoes into a greased casserole dish. Sprinkle butter and paprika on top and bake for 45 to 60 minutes.

6 Remove from oven and serve with pizzazz!

Cauliflower in Cheese Sauce

You'll Need

1   head of cauliflower, cut up
2   tablespoons cornstarch
4   cups milk
1   cup grated parmesan cheese
1   tablespoon butter

Salt to taste

Directions

1   Cut up cauliflower florets and boil in water for 5 to 10 minutes, or until soft. Place cooked cauliflower in a casserole dish.

2   Mix cornstarch into ¼ cup milk. Stir until lumps disappear and a smooth paste forms.

3   Heat remaining milk, butter, and salt in a saucepan on low heat until butter is melted. Add cornstarch paste and whisk continually while bringing sauce to a boil on medium-high heat. Mixture will thicken as it boils.

4   Once sauce is thickened, remove from heat and stir in ½ cup cheese until melted.

5   Pour white sauce over cooked cauliflower and top with remaining cheese. Broil in oven until dish is lightly brown on top.

6   Remove from oven and let cool a few minutes before serving.

Corn Cob with Lime Butter

You'll Need

4   ears of corn, shucked
3   tablespoons butter, melted
½   teaspoon grated lime peel (zest)
3   tablespoons lime juice
½   teaspoon salt
¼   teaspoon ground cayenne pepper

Directions

1 Shuck corn and place in a large pot of boiling water. Cook 7 to 8 minutes, or until bright yellow.

2 While corn is boiling, melt butter in microwave. Mix remaining ingredients into melted butter.

3 When corn is cooked, turn off heat and use tongs to remove carefully from water.

4 Brush lime butter onto corn cobs with a pastry brush.

5 Serve hot!

Hearty Meatless Minestrone

You'll Need

1 large onion, chopped
3 tablespoons olive oil
2 pieces celery, chopped
2 medium carrots, chopped
1 cup cabbage, chopped
1 medium green pepper, chopped
1 medium zucchini, chopped
6 garlic cloves, minced
3½ cups water
2 14 ½-ounce cans diced tomatoes, undrained
1 15-ounce can garbanzo beans (chickpeas), rinsed and drained
1 15-ounce can tomato puree
1 8-ounce can tomato sauce
3 tablespoons parsley flakes
2 teaspoons basil
2 teaspoons oregano
1 teaspoon salt
½ teaspoon ground black pepper
¼ teaspoon cayenne pepper
½ cup small pasta shells
  Parmesan cheese

Directions

1 Sauté onion in olive oil for 2 minutes in large pot.

2 Add celery, carrots, cabbage, green pepper, zucchini, and garlic. Sauté for 3 minutes.

3 Stir in water, tomatoes, garbanzo beans, tomato puree, tomato sauce, and seasonings. Bring to a boil.

4 Reduce heat, cover, and simmer for 15 minutes.

5 Stir in pasta and cook for 12 to 15 minutes, or until tender.

6 Garnish with cheese before serving.

From: Megan

Vegetable Chowder

You'll Need

1   tablespoon olive oil
1   medium onion, minced
3-4 cups chopped veggies
    (tomatoes, beans, carrots,
    potatoes, celery, zucchini, or
    whatever else is in refrigerator)
5   cups chicken broth
    Dash of ground black pepper
    Salt to taste
1   cup milk

Directions

1 Sauté onion in olive oil in a large soup pot until tender.

2 Add chopped vegetables and cover with chicken broth. Season with salt and pepper and simmer until vegetables are tender, about 30 to 40 minutes.

3 With an adult's help, pour soup into a blender. Mix on low. (Be careful — hot mixture will expand! If necessary, blend soup in two batches.)

4 Pour blended soup back into pot. Stir in 1 cup milk; then ladle into individual bowls to serve.

Vegetarian Chili

You'll Need

½ tablespoon canola oil
1 garlic clove, minced
1 medium onion, diced
2 carrots, diced
½ green bell pepper, chopped
1 15-ounce can kidney beans
1 15-ounce can black beans
2 tomatoes, diced
2 cups tomato juice
2 tablespoons tomato paste
1 tablespoon cumin
2 tablespoons chili powder
  Salt and pepper to taste
1 cup cooked corn kernels

Directions

1 In saucepan, sauté garlic in oil on medium heat until slightly brown.

2 Add onions, carrots, and peppers and cook until tender.

3 Stir in kidney beans and black beans, diced tomatoes, tomato juice, and tomato paste. Bring mixture to a boil on medium-high heat, and then reduce heat.

4 Add spices and simmer on low heat for 15 minutes.

5 Add corn and simmer 5 more minutes. Serve with slices of crusty bread.

From: Brenda

sweets

How sweet are your words
to my taste, sweeter than
honey to my mouth!

— Psalm 119:103

Fabulous Fudge

You'll Need

1   18-ounce bag milk chocolate chips
1   14-ounce can sweetened condensed milk
1   teaspoon vanilla extract
½   cup chopped walnuts
     8" x 8" baking pan

Directions

1 In saucepan over low heat, melt chocolate chips with sweetened condensed milk.

2 Remove from heat and stir in vanilla and walnuts.

3 Pour into 8" x 8" pan lined with wax paper.

4 Refrigerate until cool.

5 Cut into small pieces and enjoy!

From: Gwen

Best Friend Cupcakes

You'll Need

1   egg white
2   tablespoons pure maple syrup
2   tablespoons butter, melted
½   teaspoon vanilla extract
½   teaspoon almond extract
¼   cup all-purpose flour
¼   teaspoon baking powder
⅛   teaspoon salt
¼   teaspoon cinnamon
1½ tablespoons milk

Directions

1 Preheat oven to 350° Fahrenheit.

2 In bowl, whisk egg and maple syrup until combined.

3 Stir in melted butter, vanilla extract, and almond extract until combined.

4 Stir in flour, baking powder, salt, and cinnamon until smooth.

5 Stir in milk.

6 Equally divide batter between 2 greased, 4-ounce ramekins or 2 cupcake liners in a cupcake pan. If using a cupcake pan, fill remaining 10 cupcake slots half-full of water to prevent warping of pan.

7 Bake for 10 – 12 minutes, or until toothpick inserted into cake comes out clean.

8 Let cool completely before frosting.

9 Give one of the cupcakes to your best friend!

Blueberry Cake with Lemon Sauce

Blueberry Cake

You'll Need

1½ cups all-purpose flour
½ teaspoon salt
1 tablespoon baking powder
½ cup (1 stick) butter
1 cup white granulated sugar
2 eggs
⅓ cup of milk
1 teaspoon vanilla extract
1½ cups fresh blueberries

Directions

1 Preheat oven to 350° Fahrenheit and grease a 9" x 13" baking pan.

2 Mix flour, salt, and baking powder in a medium-sized bowl; set aside.

3 Cream butter and sugar together in a separate bowl. Mix in eggs and beat well to incorporate. Stir in milk and vanilla.

4 Add flour mixture and stir with spatula to combine. Gently fold in blueberries.

5 Spread batter into baking pan and bake 30 minutes.

6 Remove from oven and let cool 1 hour.

From: Lexee

Lemon Sauce

You'll Need

½ cup white granulated sugar
1 tablespoon cornstarch
⅛ teaspoon salt
¼ teaspoon nutmeg
1 cup boiling water
1 tablespoon butter
1 teaspoon grated lemon peel (zest)
Juice of one lemon

Directions

1 Combine sugar, cornstarch, salt, and nutmeg in a large saucepan. Gradually stir in boiling water; then simmer over low heat until thick, stirring occasionally.

2 Remove from heat. Stir in butter, lemon zest, and lemon juice. Serve as a topping with blueberry cake.

Lemony Lemon Bars

Crust
You'll Need

- 2 cups all-purpose flour
- 1 cup powdered sugar, plus more for dusting
  Pinch of salt
- 1 cup (2 sticks) butter, room temperature

Filling
You'll Need

- 4 eggs
- 2 cups white granulated sugar
- 6 tablespoons all-purpose flour
- 6 tablespoons fresh lemon juice
- ¼ teaspoon of grated lemon peel (zest)

Directions

1 Preheat oven to 350° Fahrenheit. Lightly grease a 9" x 13" baking pan and set aside.

2 Combine flour, powdered sugar, and salt in a large bowl.

3 Using a fork, mix in butter until mixture appears crumbly. Press mixture into pan with spatula and bake for 20 minutes.

Directions

1 Combine eggs, sugar, flour, lemon juice, and grated lemon zest in medium-sized bowl.

2 Pour filling into baked pie crust and bake 25 minutes.

3 Remove from oven and lightly sprinkle powdered sugar over filling. Let cool 1 hour before serving.

From: Molly

Butterscotch Cheesecake Bars

You'll Need

1   12-ounce package
    butterscotch chips
⅓   cup butter
2   cups graham cracker crumbs
1   cup chopped walnuts
1   8-ounce package cream
    cheese
1   14-ounce can sweetened
    condensed milk
1   teaspoon vanilla extract
1   egg

Directions

1   Preheat oven to 350° Fahrenheit and grease a
    9" x 13" baking pan.

2   In medium-sized saucepan, melt butterscotch
    chips and butter over low heat. Stir in graham
    cracker crumbs and nuts.

3   Press half of mixture firmly into bottom of
    baking pan.

4   In large mixing bowl, beat cream cheese with
    electric mixer until fluffy. Add condensed milk,
    vanilla, and egg. Mix well.

5   Pour into baking pan and top with remaining
    crumb mixture. Bake 25 to 30 minutes, or
    until toothpick inserted near center comes out
    clean.

6   Cool at room temperature; then chill in
    refrigerator 1 hour. Cut into bars. Refrigerate
    leftovers.

Chocolate Chip Cream Cheese Ball

You'll Need

1   8 ounce package cream cheese
½   cup (1 stick) butter
¼   teaspoon vanilla extract
2   tablespoons brown sugar
¾   cup powdered sugar
¾   cup mini chocolate chips
¾   cup pecans, finely chopped

Directions

1   Beat cream cheese, butter, and vanilla with electric mixer until creamy.

2   Slowly add brown sugar and powdered sugar until well blended. Stir in chocolate chips and chill 1 hour.

3   Form into ball and chill for another hour.

4   Roll cheese ball in chopped pecans. Serve with graham crackers, vanilla wafers, and other sweet cookies.

Monster Cookies

You'll Need

1   cup white granulated sugar
1   cup brown sugar
½   cup (1 stick) butter
3   eggs, beaten
1½ teaspoon vanilla extract
2   teaspoons baking soda
1½ cups peanut butter
4½ cups rolled oats
1   cup chocolate chips
1   cup hard-covered
    chocolate candies

Directions

1 Preheat oven to 350° Fahrenheit and line a cookie sheet with parchment paper.

2 Cream sugars and butter together in a large bowl. Beat eggs, add to butter mixture, and stir until incorporated.

3 Add vanilla, baking soda, and peanut butter. Mix well.

4 Stir in oatmeal, chocolate chips, and hard-covered chocolate candies.

5 Using an ice-cream scoop, drop batter onto cookie sheet. Bake 8 to 10 minutes until cookies are golden brown. Let cool on tray for 5 minutes; then place on a cooling rack.

From: Ashley

No-Bake Cookies

You'll Need

¼ cup butter

½ cup milk

2 cups white granulated sugar

1 cup semisweet chocolate chips

4 tablespoons peanut butter

3 cups rolled oats

1 teaspoon vanilla extract

Wax paper

Directions

1 Combine butter, milk, and sugar in a large saucepan and simmer over medium heat until butter is melted.

2 Bring mixture to a boil for 1 minute. Remove from heat and stir in chocolate chips, vanilla, and peanut butter until melted and thoroughly incorporated.

3 Stir in oats until thoroughly coated with mixture. Drop by spoonful onto wax paper and let cool before serving.

Oatmeal-Carrot Muffins

You'll Need

1   cup all-purpose flour
¾   cup rolled oats
1   teaspoon baking powder
¾   teaspoon baking soda
½   teaspoon salt
1¼ teaspoon ground cinnamon
½   teaspoon ground nutmeg
¾   cup brown sugar, firmly packed
⅓   cup chopped pecans (optional)
2   4-ounce jars carrot baby food
¼   cup canola oil
1   egg
½   teaspoon vanilla extract

Directions

1 Preheat oven to 400° Fahrenheit and line muffin tin with paper cupcake liners.

2 Mix dry ingredients in a large bowl.

3 Add wet ingredients and stir until mixture is moist. Batter will be orange and lumpy.

4 Pour batter into muffin tin, filling cups two-thirds full.

5 Bake for 14 to 17 minutes, or until toothpick inserted into middle of cupcake comes out clean.

6 Remove from oven and cool before serving.

From: Ellen

Delicious Chocolate Sauce

You'll Need

1   1-ounce square unsweetened chocolate
4   tablespoons butter, unsalted
¾   cup white granulated sugar
¼   teaspoon salt
½   cup milk or cream
1   teaspoon vanilla extract

Directions

1   Simmer chocolate and butter in small saucepan over low heat until melted.

2   Add sugar and salt, stirring until combined.

3   Add milk slowly, stirring as you pour.

4   Let mixture boil, stirring occasionally; then turn off heat and add vanilla.

5   Pour chocolate sauce over ice cream and enjoy!

Frosted Brownies

Brownies

You'll Need

- 1 cup white granulated sugar
- ½ cup (1 stick) butter, room temperature
- 4 eggs, beaten
- 16 ounces chocolate syrup
- 1 cup plus 1 tablespoon all-purpose flour

Directions

1 Preheat oven to 350° Fahrenheit and grease 9" x 13" baking pan.

2 Beat sugar and butter with electric mixer until light and fluffy, about 3 minutes.

3 Beat eggs; then add to butter mixture with chocolate syrup. Stir well. Mix in flour until moistened.

4 Pour batter into greased pan and bake for 25 minutes, or until a toothpick inserted near center of brownie comes out clean.

5 Remove from oven and cool slightly before frosting.

Frosting

You'll Need

- 1½ cups white granulated sugar
- 6 tablespoons butter
- 6 tablespoons milk
- ½ cup semisweet chocolate chips

Directions

1 Heat sugar, butter, and milk in a saucepan over medium heat until butter is melted.

2 Bring mixture to a boil for 40 seconds. Remove saucepan from heat.

3 Add ½ cup chocolate chips. Beat by hand until chocolate chips are melted and thoroughly incorporated.

4 Spread frosting over slightly cooled brownies, cut into squares, and serve.

Peppermint Brownies

You'll Need

1   cup (2 sticks) butter, melted
6   tablespoons cocoa
1   cup white granulated sugar
4   eggs
2   cups all-purpose flour
1 or 2 drops peppermint extract
    Candy canes

Directions

1   Preheat oven to 350° Fahrenheit and grease a 9" x 13" baking pan.

2   Melt butter in a bowl in microwave. Then combine melted butter, cocoa, and sugar in a large bowl.

3   Stir in eggs, flour, and peppermint extract. Mix well, stirring about 50 times.

4   Pour batter into greased baking pan.

5   Place candy canes into a plastic ziplock bag and seal. Lay bag on flat surface and crush candy with rolling pin or mallet. Sprinkle candy cane pieces on top of batter.

6   Bake for 30 minutes. Remove from oven and cool; then cut into squares and enjoy!

Coated Ice Cream with Hot Chocolate

Ice-Cream Balls

You'll Need

- Wax paper
- ¼ cup peanut butter
- 1 cup graham cracker crumbs
- 2 teaspoons white granulated sugar
- ¼ teaspoon ground cinnamon
- 1 quart vanilla ice cream

Directions

1. Cover a cookie sheet or jelly-roll pan with wax paper.

2. Mix peanut butter, graham-cracker crumbs, sugar, and cinnamon in medium-sized bowl.

3. Working quickly, form ice cream into balls and roll in peanut butter mixture until evenly coated.

4. Place coated ice cream balls on cookie sheet and store in freezer until ready to eat.

Hot Chocolate Topping

You'll Need

- 1 cup white granulated sugar
- 1 cup water
- 3 level tablespoons cornstarch
- 2 tablespoons cocoa
- 1 teaspoon vanilla extract
- 1 tablespoon butter
- Dash of salt

Directions

1. Combine sugar, water, cornstarch, and cocoa in a saucepan over medium heat. Stir until mixture thickens.

2. Remove from heat and add vanilla, butter, and salt, stirring until butter melts.

3. Serve hot over ice cream balls.

holidays

On this mountain the LORD Almighty will prepare a feast of rich food for all peoples, a banquet of aged wine — the best of meats and the finest of wines.

—Isaiah 25:6

Sparkling New Year's Punch

You'll Need

½ cup white granulated sugar
1½ cups water
½ cup orange juice
2 cups cranberry juice
1 cup pineapple juice
2 2-liter bottles of lemon-lime soda

Directions

1 Combine sugar, water, and juices in punch bowl.

2 Add soda just before serving.

3 Serve in fluted glasses.

Chocolate Truffles

You'll Need

2   ounces bittersweet chocolate
¼   cup heavy cream
1   tablespoon powdered sugar
1   teaspoon vanilla extract
1   cup cocoa powder, toasted chopped
    nuts, or toasted coconut

Directions

1 Place chocolate, heavy cream, sugar, and vanilla in a microwave-safe bowl.

2 Microwave on high for 20 – 30 seconds.

3 Stir until smooth.

4 Refrigerate for 1 hour.

5 Scoop out teaspoonfuls and roll into balls.

6 Roll balls in cocoa powder, nuts, or coconut.

7 Share with someone you love.

Berries and Cherries

You'll Need

Fresh strawberries
Maraschino cherries with stems
Semisweet chocolate chips
Wax paper
Sprinkles (optional)

Directions

1 Wash strawberries; drain on paper towel.

2 Place cherries on paper towel to drain.

3 Microwave chocolate chips, ½ cup at a time, on medium power for 30 seconds. Stir. Repeat until chocolate is melted and smooth.

4 Dip each piece of fruit into melted chocolate to coat. Place dipped fruit on wax paper. If desired, add colorful sprinkles. Allow chocolate to harden.

5 Remove from wax paper and serve immediately.

Traditional Irish Soda Bread

You'll Need

4	cups all-purpose flour
4	tablespoons white granulated sugar
1	teaspoon baking soda
1	tablespoon baking powder
½	teaspoon salt
½	cup butter, softened
1¼	cup buttermilk
1	egg
¼	cup butter, melted

Directions

1 Preheat oven to 375° Fahrenheit. Lightly grease a baking sheet.

2 Mix flour, sugar, baking soda, baking powder, salt, and butter in a large bowl.

3 Stir in 1 cup of buttermilk and egg.

4 Place dough on a lightly floured surface and knead slightly.

5 Form dough into a ball and place on greased baking sheet.

6 In a small bowl, combine melted butter with ¼ cup buttermilk.

7 Brush dough with butter mixture.

8 Use a sharp knife to cut an X into top of loaf.

9 Bake for 45 to 50 minutes, or until a toothpick inserted into center of loaf comes out clean.

10 Remove from oven and cool on wire rack.

11 Slice and serve with butter and a bowl of stew!

Green Shamrock Punch

You'll Need

2 packages lemon-lime powdered drink mix

2 quarts water

1½ cups white granulated sugar

1 46-ounce can pineapple juice

1 2-liter bottle ginger ale

½ gallon lime sherbet

Directions

1 Mix powdered drink mix, water, sugar, and pineapple juice in a punch bowl.

2 Add ginger ale and sherbet just before serving.

Saint Patrick's Salad

You'll Need

1 chopped green apple
2 tablespoons chopped
   pistachios (optional)
1 tablespoon sunflower seeds
¼ cup plain yogurt
1 tablespoon honey
   Salad greens

Directions

1 Mix all ingredients, except salad greens, in a medium-sized bowl.

2 Cover bowl with plastic wrap and chill in refrigerator for 1 hour.

3 Serve apple mixture on a bed of salad greens and enjoy!

From: Haley

Hot Cross Buns

Dough
You'll Need
2	tablespoons active, dry yeast
½	cup warm water
1	cup warm milk
½	cup white granulated sugar
¼	cup butter, softened
1	teaspoon salt
½	teaspoon vanilla extract
½	teaspoon ground cinnamon
½	teaspoon ground nutmeg
1	cup raisins
6½	cups all-purpose flour
4	eggs

Egg Wash
You'll Need
2	tablespoons cold water
1	egg yolk

Frosting
You'll Need
1	cup powdered sugar
1	tablespoon milk or water
½	teaspoon vanilla extract

Directions

1 Dissolve yeast in warm water. Stir in milk, sugar, butter, salt, vanilla, cinnamon, nutmeg, raisins, and 4 cups of flour. Beat until smooth.

2 Continue to stir, adding one egg at a time.

3 Mix in remaining flour to form soft dough.

4 Place dough on lightly floured surface and knead for about 5 minutes, until dough is smooth and elastic.

5 Put dough in a greased bowl, cover, and let rise until double in size, approximately 1 hour.

6 Then punch dough down and divide it into halves.

7 Make 15 balls out of each half of dough. Place balls about 2 inches apart on lightly greased baking sheets.

8 Carefully cut a cross on top of each ball of dough (or bun). Cover buns and let rise until they double in size.

9 While buns rise, preheat oven to 375° Fahrenheit. Mix water and egg yolk in a small bowl.

10 Brush tops of buns with egg-and-water mixture.

11 Bake for 15 to 18 minutes. Remove from oven and let buns cool.

12 Mix powdered sugar, water, and vanilla and paint crosses on each roll with frosting.

Deviled Eggs

Directions

1 Place six eggs in a single layer in a saucepan.

2 Cover eggs with cold water so that water is an inch or two above eggs.

3 Put saucepan on stove on high heat, and bring water to boil.

4 When water begins to boil, reduce heat to low.

5 Let simmer for one minute, then remove pan from heat.

6 Cover saucepan and let sit for 12 minutes.

7 Remove eggs from water and let cool.

8 When eggs are cool, remove shells.

9 Cut eggs in half lengthwise and scoop out yolks.

10 Mash yolks in small bowl.

11 Blend in vinegar, mayonnaise, mustard, salt, and pepper. Add more mayonnaise if mixture seems too dry.

12 Evenly divide yolk mixture back into halved egg whites.

13 Sprinkle with paprika.

You'll Need

6 eggs
1 teaspoon white vinegar
1 tablespoon mayonnaise
¼ teaspoon prepared mustard
salt and pepper to taste
1 teaspoon paprika

Crispy Easter Nests

You'll Need

1 7-ounce jar of marshmallow crème

¼ cup creamy peanut butter

2 tablespoons butter, melted

1 cup candy-coated chocolates

2 cups puffed rice cereal

Jelly beans or small chocolate eggs

Directions

1 Combine marshmallow crème, peanut butter, and melted butter.

2 Add chocolates and cereal.

3 Drop by ⅓ cup onto greased cookie sheet.

4 With buttered hands, form into nest shapes.

5 Fill nest with jelly beans and small chocolate egg candies.

6 Let cool before eating.

Red, White, and Blue Fruit Shake

You'll Need

- 2 cups milk
- ⅔ cup frozen strawberries
- ⅔ cup frozen raspberries
- ⅔ cup blueberries
- 2 tablespoons of frozen orange juice concentrate
- 2 tablespoons of yogurt (plain or flavored)
- 2 tablespoons of maple syrup
- Whipped cream (optional)

Directions

1 Pour all ingredients except whipped cream into a blender.

2 Blend until smooth.

3 Pour into a large glass and top with whipped cream.

From: Kyria

Strawberry-Lemon Popsicles

Directions

1 Heat lemon juice in microwave for 45 seconds.

2 Mix with ¼ cup sugar and stir until sugar dissolves.

3 Whisk in 1 cup yogurt until smooth.

4 Refrigerate.

5 Place strawberries, water, and remaining ¼ cup sugar in medium saucepan and bring to a boil. Simmer for five minutes.

6 Pour strawberries and 1 teaspoon lemon juice into a blender and pulse until pureed.

7 Chill in refrigerator until cool.

8 Whisk remaining 1 cup yogurt into strawberry mixture until smooth.

9 Spoon alternating layers of lemon- and strawberry-yogurt mix into paper cups.

10 Stick a popsicle stick into each filled cup.

11 Freeze overnight.

12 To serve, peel off paper cup and enjoy!

You'll Need

¼ cup fresh lemon juice
½ cup white sugar
2 cups yogurt, plain or vanilla flavored
1 pint strawberries, hulled
2 tablespoons water
1 teaspoon lemon juice
Small paper cups
Popsicle sticks

Show-Your-Colors Mini Cheesecakes

You'll Need

8   ounces cream cheese, softened
⅓   cup powdered sugar
1   teaspoon vanilla extract
1   teaspoon grated lemon peel (zest)
2   cups whipped topping
1   box vanilla wafers
     Strawberry or cherry topping
     Blueberries (optional)
     Cupcake liners

Directions

1 In a large bowl, combine cream cheese, powdered sugar, vanilla, and lemon zest. Beat with electric mixer until fluffy (about 2 minutes).

2 Fold whipped topping into cheese mixture.

3 Place 1 vanilla wafer in bottom of each cupcake liner.

4 Divide cheese mixture into cupcake liners and chill in refrigerator.

5 Before serving, add fruit topping to each cheesecake cup.

Pumpkin Bread

You'll Need

3½ cups all-purpose flour

2 teaspoons baking soda

1½ teaspoon salt

½ teaspoon baking powder

3 cups white granulated sugar

1 cup vegetable oil

4 eggs

⅔ cup water

1 15-ounce can pumpkin puree

2 teaspoons ground ginger

1 teaspoon ground allspice

1 teaspoon ground cinnamon

1 teaspoon ground cloves

Directions

1 Preheat oven to 350° Fahrenheit and lightly grease two 9" x 5" loaf pans.

2 In a medium bowl, combine flour, baking soda, salt, and baking powder; set aside.

3 In a large mixing bowl, combine sugar, oil, and eggs; beat until smooth. Add water and beat until well blended. Stir in pumpkin, ginger, allspice, cinnamon, and cloves.

4 Add flour mixture and stir to combine. Divide batter between two greased pans and bake for 1 hour, or until a toothpick inserted near center of bread comes out clean.

5 Cool 1 hour before serving.

From: Baylee

Count-Your-Blessings Cornucopia

You'll Need

2   6-inch flour tortillas
1   small can baby corn
    Small carrots, peeled
    Grape tomatoes
    Pea pods
    Black olives
    Celery sticks
    Ranch dressing or dip

Directions

1   Cut tortillas in half. Each half makes one cornucopia.

2   Spread a thin layer of ranch dressing or dip on tortilla halves.

3   Starting on straight side of each tortilla, roll into cone shape and place seam side down on a plate.

4   Fill each cornucopia with your favorite veggies and serve with ranch dressing or dip.

5   Before each bite, name a blessing God has filled your life with this year!

Thanksgiving Muffins

Muffins
You'll Need

1   large sweet potato
2½ cups all-purpose flour
1½ teaspoons baking powder
½   teaspoon salt
¼   teaspoon baking soda
¼   teaspoon ground nutmeg
¼   cup buttermilk
⅓   cup milk
1   tablespoon sour cream
1   teaspoon vanilla extract
1   stick unsalted butter,
    room temperature
¾   cup brown sugar
2   eggs

Topping
You'll Need

4   tablespoons butter
½   cup white
    granulated sugar
2   teaspoons ground
    cinnamon

Directions

1 Preheat oven to 400° Fahrenheit.

2 Wash sweet potato and prick all over with fork.

3 Wrap sweet potato in tin foil and bake for 30 – 40 minutes or until insides are soft.

4 Remove from oven and let cool.

5 When cooled, cut sweet potato in half and scrape out insides. Mash until all lumps are gone

6 Mix buttermilk, milk, mashed sweet potato, sour cream, and vanilla extract in a bowl.

7 Mix flour, baking powder, salt, baking soda, and ground nutmeg in another bowl.

8 In large mixing bowl, cream butter and brown sugar with electric mixer. Add eggs one at a time. Alternately mix dry and wet ingredients into butter-sugar mixture, starting and ending with dry; mix only until each addition is incorporated.

9 Grease muffin pan and fill with batter.

10 Bake in a 350° Fahrenheit oven for 20 minutes, or until a toothpick inserted into a muffin comes out clean.

11 Melt butter in saucepan.

12 Mix cinnamon and sugar.

13 Dip top of muffin in melted butter and then roll in cinnamon-sugar.

Simple Corn Soufflé

You'll Need

1 large egg
1 stick of butter, melted
1 15-ounce can whole kernel corn, drained
1 15-ounce can creamed corn
1 8½-ounce box corn muffin mix
1 cup of sour cream
  1½-quart oven-safe dish

Directions

1 Preheat oven to 400° Fahrenheit.

2 Mix all ingredients together in large mixing bowl.

3 Pour mixture into 1½-quart oven-safe dish and bake for 45 to 60 minutes.

4 Soufflé is done when it has risen slightly and is lightly brown on top.

5 Serve immediately.

From: Beth

Cathedral Window Cookies

You'll Need

1   package sugar-cookie dough

4   rolls or 5-ounce package hard candy in various colors

    2 ½- to 3-inch cookie cutters

    1-inch cookie cutters

    Plastic ziplock bags

Directions

1. Sort candy by colors into plastic ziplock bags and seal. Place each bag on flat surface and crush candy with a rolling pin or mallet.

2. Preheat oven to 375° Fahrenheit and line two cookie sheets with parchment paper or aluminum foil.

3. Roll out prepackaged cookie dough on a lightly floured surface.

4. Cut out wide shapes in dough with large cookie cutters. Place cookies 1 inch apart on cookie sheets.

5. Use smaller cookie cutter to cut out a design from center of each cookie. Hearts, triangles, and circles work well.

6. With a spoon, carefully fill cutouts with crushed candy. Try not to get candy on dough.

7. For tree ornaments, use a straw to make a small hole in top of each cookie.

8. Bake 7 to 9 minutes, until candy is melted and cookies are firm and beginning to brown around edges. Watch carefully so candy doesn't burn.

9. Remove cookies from oven and cool until candy is hard.

10. Gently remove foil or parchment from back of cookies. To make tree ornaments, insert ribbon through hole at top.

Cranberry Almond Loaves

You'll Need

- 4 cups all-purpose flour
- 1 cup white granulated sugar
- 4 teaspoons baking powder
- 2 teaspoons salt
- 2 eggs
- 1 cup milk
- 1 cup (2 sticks) butter, melted
- 4 teaspoons almond extract
- 2 6-ounce packages dried cranberries
- 2 tablespoons white granulated sugar (for topping)
- ½ cup sliced almonds
- Green or red cellophane wrap (optional)

Directions

1 Preheat oven to 350° Fahrenheit and grease 2 loaf pans.

2 Combine flour, sugar, baking powder, and salt in large bowl.

3 Mix eggs, milk, butter, almond extract, and dried cranberries in separate bowl. Add to dry ingredients; stir until moist.

4 Divide batter evenly between loaf pans. Sprinkle with sugar and almonds.

5 Bake for 1 hour, or until a toothpick inserted near center of loaf comes out clean.

6 Remove loaves from oven and cool. Wrap in cellophane and give to family and friends.

Wacky Gingerbread Men

You'll Need

½ cup (1 stick) butter
½ cup brown sugar
3¼ cups all-purpose flour
1 teaspoon salt
1 teaspoon baking soda
½ teaspoon ground cinnamon

½ teaspoon ground ginger
¾ cup molasses
¼ cup water
Mini hard-covered chocolate candies
Hard cinnamon candies
Decorator frosting

Directions

1 Preheat oven to 350° Fahrenheit and lightly grease a cookie sheet.

2 Cream together butter and sugar in a large bowl.

3 Combine flour, salt, soda, and spices in separate bowl. Then gradually add flour mixture, molasses, and water to creamed butter. Mix thoroughly.

4 Chill for an hour or more in refrigerator.

5 On floured surface, roll dough to ¼-inch thick and, using a knife, cut out gingerbread men. Get creative and make snowboarders, surfers, or other wacky gingerbread men.

6 Place dough cutouts on cookie sheet. Use candies to give gingerbread men eyes and mouths.

7 Bake at 350° for 12–15 minutes.

8 Remove from oven and place on cooling rack. When cookies are cool, use frosting to add hair, clothes, and hats.

Christmas Swirl Cookies

You'll Need

2 cups all-purpose flour

½ teaspoon baking powder

⅔ cup powdered sugar

¼ cup white granulated sugar

1¼ cup butter, room temperature and cut into chunks

1 teaspoon vanilla

½ teaspoon red or green food coloring

½ teaspoon peppermint extract

1 tablespoon flour

Pastry brush

1½ cup red and green sprinkles

Directions

1 With mixer, combine 2 cups flour, baking powder, and sugars until well blended.

2 Gradually add butter and vanilla extract until dough forms into a ball.

3 Remove dough and divide into two equal parts.

4 Return one part to mixer bowl and add food coloring and peppermint extract. If dough is too wet, add 1 tablespoon flour.

5 Roll out each portion of dough between two sheets of wax paper until each is 11" long, 9" inches wide, and ¼" thick.

6 Slide both rolled-out portions onto cookie sheets and chill in refrigerator for 2 hours.

7 When firm, remove from refrigerator and remove top sheets of wax paper from both portions.

8 Brush uncolored dough lightly with water using a pastry brush.

9 Flip colored dough onto uncolored dough so they are evenly stacked on top of each other.

10 Seal edges by pressing them together.

11 Beginning with the long side, roll dough into a log.

12 Pour sprinkles onto a large platter.

13 Gently lift log onto sprinkles and roll log in sprinkles until the log is completely covered.

14 Wrap sprinkle-covered log in plastic wrap and place in refrigerator for 4 hours.

15 Remove from refrigerator and slice dough into ¼-inch slices.

16 Place slices on greased baking sheets.

17 Bake at 350° Fahrenheit for 15–17 minutes, or until edges are slightly golden.

18 Let the cookies cool on baking sheet for 5 minutes, then move to a wire rack to finish cooling.

Index

Faithgirlz Handbook

How to let your faith shine through

Suzanne Hadley

What does it really mean to be a Faithgirl? The *Faithgirlz! Handbook* contains ideas and activities to help bring girls and their friends closer to God and more in touch with his Word.

Softcover: 978-0-310-726975

Available in stores and online!

Faithgirlz Journal

My Doodles, Dreams, and Devotions

Just Between You and God

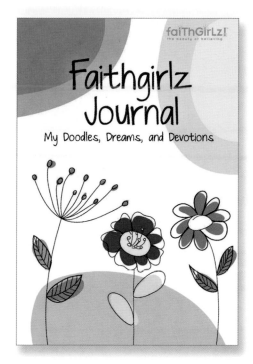

Looking for a place to dream, doodle, and record your inner-most questions and secrets? You will find what you seek within the pages of the *Faithgirlz Journal,* which has plenty of space for you to discover who you are, explore who God is shaping you to be, or write down whatever inspires you. Each journal page has awesome quotes and powerful Bible verses to encourage you on your walk with God! So grab a pen, colored pencils, or even a handful of markers. Whatever you write is just between you and God.

Hardcover: 978-0-310-72587-9

Available in stores and online!

NIV Faithgirlz! Backpack Bible,
Revised Edition

Small enough to fit into a backpack or bag, this Bible can go anywhere a girl does.

Features include:

- Fun Italian Duo-Tone™ design
- Twelve full-color pages of Faithgirlz fun that helps girls learn the "Beauty of Believing!"
- Words of Christ in red
- Ribbon marker
- Complete text of the bestselling NIV translation

Italian Duo-Tone™, Pink: 978-0-310-72228-1

Available in stores and online!

Other Books in the Faithgirlz! Series

NIV Faithgirlz! Bible,
Revised Edition

NANCY RUE

Every girl wants to know she's totally unique and special.

This Bible says that with Faithgirlz! sparkle. Through the many in-text features found only in the *Faithgirlz! Bible,* girls will grow closer to God as they discover the journey of a lifetime.

Features include:

- Book introductions—Read about the who, when, where, and what of each book.
- Dream Girl—Use your imagination to put yourself in the story.
- Bring It On!—Take quizzes to really get to know yourself.
- Is There a Little (Eve, Ruth, Isaiah) in You?—See for yourself what you have in common.
- Words to Live By—Check out these Bible verses that are great for memorizing.
- What Happens Next?—Create a list of events to tell a Bible story in your own words.
- Oh, I Get It!—Find answers to Bible questions you've wondered about.
- The complete NIV translation
- Features written by bestselling author Nancy Rue

Hardcover: 978-0-310-72236-6

Available in stores and online!

FOCUS ON THE FAMILY®

Hungry for More?

Many of the recipes in this book come from the pages of *Focus on the Family Clubhouse* magazine. For twenty-five years, *Clubhouse* has provided fun recipes, entertaining crafts, and hilarious stories that help kids (eight- to twelve-years-old) grow in Christ. We can't wait to show you what we've got cooking every month!

Subscribe to *Clubhouse* magazine and learn about our magazine for younger kids at FocusOnTheFamily.com/magazines

Or call us at 800-A-FAMILY (232-6459)

Join the Club!

We want to hear from you. Please send your comments about this book to us in care of zreview@zondervan.com. Thank you.

ZONDERVAN.com/
AUTHORTRACKER
follow your favorite authors